LIGHT STREAM

SPIRIT INSPIRED POETRY AND POETIC PROSE

ROBERT JAMES SCHOUT

SCHOUT IT OUT PUBLISHING

Light Stream

Spirit Inspired Poetry and Poetic Prose

Publisher
Schout It Out LLC: Schout It Out Publishing
Wilmington, Delaware

ISBN: 978-1-959168-12-6

Library of Congress Control Number: 2024915405

First Edition

For more information about the author and other books and products by Robert James Schout and Schout It Out LLC, visit: www.schoutitout.com

To order copies of this book in digital, hardcopy, or audio formats, visit: www.schoutitout.com

ACKNOWLEDGMENTS

To my high school poetry teachers, friends, and those in my
Unity family, each of whom has helped me fall in love with
poetry and reminded me to turn inward for wisdom.

Special gratitude is given to
Wanda Zamorano, Margie Hornick, and the late Ed Townley.
Each one has been a messenger of Spirit, constantly reminding
me that light, love, and presence are constants in life. Goodness
is everywhere present. All answers can be found
within if we just stop, look, and listen in stillness.

We must always remember the truth.
Each one of us is, without reservation or precondition,
a stream of light within this world.

INTRODUCTION

The *Light Stream* book of poetry and poetic prose is not meant to entreat you, the reader, to pray, to preach, to beseech, or to praise. Its sole purpose is to inspire, enlighten, and invite three things: contemplation, meditation, and revelation of assurance, peace, and love within and around you.

Whoever and whatever you turn to in faith, whether it be during times of need, in despair, in gratitude, for healing energy, or for intuitive wisdom, you do so with a sense of knowing, to seek a sense of presence, to dwell within mindfulness, with a hope that there is a source that will sustain you. This universal presence does not need, want, nor desire praise, preaching, begging nor beseeching. When we do so, we are being ever so human. Bestowing human frailties and characteristics upon something that we are a part of, but which is far beyond human comprehension. We are calling out for some light – hope, assurance, peace, remedy, knowledge – that is already available and often inside of ourselves. We forget fundamental truths that are revealed around us and within us. All we need to do is stop, look, listen, acknowledge, and act with true love, not false praise nor platitudes.

Light Stream poems and poetic prose passages remind us to observe and acknowledge, affirm and be assured, listen and change, progress and act in accordance with the light of love's invitations and manifestations: beauty, peace, kindness, understanding, compassion-in-action, happiness-in-heart. To connect with this stream of presence, power, and light within and around us, we meditate, grow in awareness, sit in wonder, express unending gratitude for that which is always available, and follow its wisdom. Most importantly, we listen and allow this light (i.e., this energy, this Source, this God/god, this wisdom, Mother, Presence, this love, these answers) to stream in and through us.

Light, with its infinite power of peace, healing, strength, and softness, will always stream to, in, around, and through you. It is happening now and in constant occurrence. It is the nature of Light. Just as the sun always shines regardless of whether it is nighttime for you; there is daylight somewhere else. Regardless of whether there are storm clouds overhead and skies remain gray. The sun is still shining above the clouds. Whether you benefit from the Light depends on your willingness and daily practice of acting in accordance with the wisdom found in the Light; not simply from acknowledging the presence of or proselytizing about the Light. As you settle into stillness, choose to see light in everyone and everything, and strive to receive the continual unfoldment of enlightenment within, the streams of light refract and expand within your heart and mind. They enter every cell of your body.

Light Stream is divided into three parts: Truth Told, Invitations to Journey Within, and Gifts from Standing in the Light.

The free-form poems of *Light Stream* are not religious, nor do they represent a particular spiritual path. The light of love, light of compassion, light of wisdom streams to every person, every being, and everything, everywhere at every moment, without exception and without condition. That is the Truth. No matter what religious, spiritual, or philosophical path you are on, or if you take no path at all, it does not matter. Total love, total wisdom, and a guarantee of total assurance are present to everyone, everywhere, requiring no need to affiliate with a faith or particular path. Light – Presence – is universal. Dogma and doctrine must always be pushed aside, as curtains must be, to allow natural light to steam in and fill living spaces.

It does not matter what you call your Light source: God, Buddha, Allah, Mother, Gaia, Presence, energy, source, etc. Use words that bring comfort to you. As you read or listen to the poems and prose from *Light Stream*, dwell in the inner space of your source of light. Your awareness, your ecstasy of experience, your journey to enlightenment, your revelations are yours alone. Make your path personal, for Light illuminates everything. That which is revealed by Light may be unique to each person. When you turn within or see without, choosing only to look through the lens of love, understanding, beauty, and compassion, then Light will stream into you and move through you, and you, too, will become a stream of light for this world.

-    Robert J. Schout

CONTENTS

PART I

TRUTH TOLD

COME, DEAR ONE

Come

Dear one

Live in your love

Dive into your hopes

Bury yourself in dreams

Let these be your reality

Feel your heart enfolded

Let your hands be filled

Think the thoughts that

Convince me, you are

And I will do the rest

Let me give to you

All you desire

Come dear

One

THE PROMISE

My love is eternal, always present,
     always here, always within you,
     never diminished,
     never deterred,
     never dimmed.

My love,
     let it touch you,
     transform you,
     with your head and heart
     transfixed on Spirit within.

Feel Its power.
     become aware of eternal presence.
     know your purpose.
     sense that which you embody.
     let it expand within you, express through you.

It is I,
     faith, joy, peace
     wisdom, father, mother
     love, expressing as Oneness
     within and without.

This is my love,
     your love, all love,
     the only love that you will ever need,
     that you truly desire,
     that exists.

Turn to me.
> turn within.
> there you will find me,
> find yourself,
> find love.

There,
> in the silence,
> in the stillness
> there is love,
> there am I.

I Am Here

I Am Here
To offer shelter
To offer hope
To offer peace
To offer love
To offer wisdom
To offer insight
For Family
For Friends
For Strangers
For Enemies
For Everyone
For Everything
For You
In every face
In every form
In every desire
In every tear
In every triumph
In every idea
In every effort
I Am Here

I AM

You do not see me, but know that I Am.
You can hear me. This is enough to calm an anxious mind.
You can feel me. This is enough to tender a steeled heart.
You can sense me. This is enough to enlighten a shadowed mind.
Simply remember that I Am.

Perfection incarnate.
There can be nothing else, if you let me be.
No disease will remain rooted in mind. No wound cannot be healed.
No question left unanswered. No dream unfulfilled.
If you believe, I Am.

I Am power beyond description, yet present in every touch.
I Am knowing beyond all knowledge, yet present in every thought.
I Am presence and life itself, that which animates and lives in all.
All is birthed and transformed by me. All exists in me and as me.
For, I Am All.

I do not need praise nor preaching.
I do not need beckoning nor beseeching.
Your proselytizing and evangelizing matter not to me.
I am and express regardless of what you say or do. None are beholden.
For all are and is already a part of me and will always be.

I take no sides except the sides of love, peace, and healing.
If a side I must take then it will be the side that sustains
the mountains and seas, the skies and trees,
the beings alive in this world and others.
Remember, I was here before and will always be forever more.

I Am everywhere. I Am everything:
every wish, every thought, every desire,
every form of life that ever was, is, and will be.
Call me, touch me, feel me, seize me, grasp hold of my mind,
let my spirit unfurl in and enfold you, and you will know that,

I Am

WHAT LIES BEHIND

Behind every leaf,
It is.

Under every rock,
It lies.

Animating everything,
It moves.

Beneath every thought,
It creates.

Before a word is spoken,
It whispers.

In every life form,
It dwells.

In everything,
It is.

ETERNAL CONNECTION

Like a wave unto the ocean,
and a raindrop unto a storm.
Like a grain of sand unto a beach.
It is simply a matter of form.

Like a ray of light unto sunrise,
and mist unto a cloud.
Like a smile on a face,
or a voice in a crowd.

Like plants unto a forest,
and birds unto a tree.
Like fish unto the water.
I am unto thee.

Like blood unto the body.
Like thoughts unto the mind.
Like feelings of the heart.
I am each and every kind.

So, you are unto me,
a part of the great expanse,
a part of a greater love,
a part of a greater dance.

You are the echo of my voice,
the beating of my heart,
the action of my hands,
of this you are a part.

Know we are never separate.
know that we can never part.
Know that we are always one,
in body, mind and heart.

RAPTUROUS LOVE

Yearning.
My heart burning for thee.
I want to be taken in your arms.
                    Hold me and mold me.

You are all that I think about.
All of my wants, needs, and desires
are wrapped up
                    in you.

One moment with you
satisfies a lifetime of desire.
My thirst is unquenchable.
                    I drink of life itself.

I want to give myself to you;
give you my heart, my soul,
my life, my love.
                    You are my everything.

And I want the same. No, more.
I want to know you, explore you,
discover you,
                    To understand your depth.

I see you all around me,
everywhere I go.
I cannot, nor wish to escape.
                    Your presence is to breathe.

What is this hold that you
have over me?
This prison of love that
                    I want never to escape.

I give my life to you.
Use me, as you see fit.
Twist me, turn me, shape me into
                    your desire.

I shall bend but not break.
I contort in your caress.
I feel the gentle comfort of
                    your tender hands.

I give you my body, my voice, my mind.
Sculpt them into your intended perfect form
that I may be a reflection of you and
                    be familiar to all.

Do this so that I may be desirable, pleasing, and provocative
enticing kindred spirits to look and listen.
Inviting to you, the hearts and minds of millions
                    enraptured by love.

Let me seduce them with your words,
enrapture them with your spirit, enfold
them with your light and
                    I will bring them home.

I will share with them, care for them,
Help them release fears and love,
Deliver them tenderly
                    to your sweet embrace.

Kiss me with the early morning dawn.
Fill me with the passion of heavenly bliss.
Treat me to the ecstasy of your love
                    that I and all

may walk this day, hand in hand,
living in your heart
dwelling this day and forevermore
                    with you.

LIGHT STREAM

Light stream, flood my consciousness with peace.
My mind, awash with crisp, gentle, clarity.
The wisdom of the universe flowing within
All knowing that ever was and ever will be,
     Mine in a moment.
          Truth unfolds.

Light streams, rushing through the tributaries of my mind and heart.
Collecting, pooling in a well that reaches into the Earth and beyond.
Beckoning me to immerse myself in its flow
Reaching out cupping with my hands, joy itself
     Lifted to my lips,
          To quench lifetimes of thirst.

Flow, light stream, flow. Meander your way to my soul.
Let not the banks nor boundaries that I have erected, hoping to control
your direction and my destiny, contain your power.
Rush through the caverns and canyons of my fear,
     Tearing at their walls.
          Carving new pathways for light to flow.

Wash over them until they crumble beneath your mighty power.
Send wave after wave of light, streaming into my life from infinity.
For I wish to bath in cool waters and bask in warmth.
Filling myself, dissolving myself, until I radiate love.
     Then I, too, for this world,
          will become a stream of light.

THE ESSENCE OF RAPTURE

Hold me and mold me.

In you,

I drink of life itself.

You are my everything.

To understand your depth.

Your presence is to breathe.

I want never to escape

your desire,

your tender hands.

Be familiar to all,

enraptured by love.

I will bring them home

to your sweet embrace,

that I and all will be with you.

MY GIFT TO THEE

My gift to thee is this.

To be a gift the world may see
knowing in depth what all can be.

To be the one that will transcend
unfounded fears that always bend,

the minds of men away from thee
and blind their hearts, unable to see,

the truth and promise of life foretold
of thee within, to have and hold.

My gift to thee and to this world
is to live the truth, spirit unfurled.

That all may see what they can be,
the truth and light, one with thee.

TRUST

One day the world may end,
but, on this, my love, depend.
I will love you when days are gone,
Love you lifetimes long,
With a love promised to transcend,

across time and space,
I make this central case,
though others cannot conceive,
 only you need believe.
Rest assured in this state of grace,

that my love will last, though all may die.
Trust in this, as days go by,
that through it all my love will bear
all pain and laughter, hope and prayer,
till evening comes and morning's nye.

There may be tumult and turmoil
as may others embroil,
extolling fear and sadness
anger and madness.
Still, be steadfastly loyal,

to your heart and soul, and see each sign
appear in you, a simple design.
Bound by love, in ecstasy.
Trust and believe to be set free
and experience the presence of the divine.

TRUTH

Spirit breathes
Cells speak
Bodies react
Worlds reborn

I Am In Reality

Do you not see, my child,
the light that glows so brightly in your eyes?
      It is my light, in you!

Do you not feel the love that flows
with a constancy into your heart?
      It is my love, filling you!

Do you not hear the assurances of truth
that dwell in your mind?
      They are my words that heal, and ideas that grow, in you!

Do you not witness the beings of the air,
the soiled plants, the churning seas?
      I am in everything and everywhere!

Do you not sense my presence in every person
across cultures and continents?
      I am in everyone!

Do you not trust the gentleness of my arms,
as I hold you in times of trouble?
      I am your comfort and shelter!

Do you not realize that all words,
entreating you to kindness, come from my heart?
      I am compassion in life!

Do you not hear the whisper of my voice,
calling out to you in the night?
        I am at your side seeing you safely thru 'til dawn!

Do you not know that I can
never abandon you nor anyone?
        I am omnipresence itself.

I am, in reality, in you, in all,
around you, as you,
            in all ways, always!

WE ARE ONE

We are One. One in body. One in mind.
One in spirit. Our union enshrined.

We are one in hand and one in heart.
One in love, never apart.

We are one in thought, listen to me,
one in body and you will see,

that the oneness of being brings gifts so rare,
oneness of thinking, allows you to hear.

Our oneness of heart allows me to give,
all that you ask for as long as you live.

Let oneness be in heart and in mind,
open your hands to receive every kind,

of blessing meant to be bestowed upon you,
blessings of love and abundance too;

blessings of wealth and material and friends,
blessings so grand, so hard to comprehend;

blessings that so easily fall in hand,
a blessing you are, please understand.

This is my promise, my guarantee
for we are One, you and me.

PART II

INVITATIONS TO JOURNEY WITHIN

REST AWHILE

Slow down dear one, and rest a while

at my side

In the midst of your frantic, frenetic pace,
life passes you by
and will end,

all too soon

So, stop, dear one, and rest awhile.
Sit a moment by my side
and notice with me,

the bliss of simply being.

The colors of the sky,
the early morning dew,
the sounds of life

surrounding you.

The silence of the trees,
the turning of the tide,
the freshness of a breeze

at my side.

All is missed,
as you speed on by,
So, sit dear one and

rest awhile.

GOD'S ANSWER

I asked in the silence:
  God, what is it that you want from me?

And from the silence, a voice was heard:
To simply BE...
all that you want to be, all that's inside of me,
all that you hope, striving to grow,
all that I Am, is all you will know.

Life expresses in every sight and sound.
Release control, let happiness abound.
See me in joy wherever you go.
Experience my love and truly know,

heaven is here, right now, for you,
abundance guaranteed, in all you do.
For that which I Am is all you conceive,
all you desire and are willing to receive.

What I want from you is simply this,
to accept life's gentle, tender kiss.
What I want from you is to simply be,
exploring, discovering, the essence, of Me.

WHAT GOOD IS

What good is the wealth of the world,
if I cannot buy peace?

What good is donning clothes woven from the most expensive fabrics,
if I cannot see the beauty inside?

What good is being the master of many servants,
if I cannot master the art of love?

What good is owning many homes,
if the house of the self is left in disarray, rotting under foot?

What good is drinking the finest wines,
if I am not intoxicated by life itself?

For what good is,
must be found in me.

Go!

Go into the silence and you shall know all that I know.
the wisdom of the ages and sages lie in wait before thee.

Go into the silence that lies within and you will know
how to live, how grow, how to love, how to sow,

> Seeds of peace and seeds of hope,
> beyond the scope of human knowing.

It is in the silence that you shall know.

So, go!

DRINK

My Beloved

Drink from the chalice of love.
Every drop opens one's eyes, cleanses one's heart, clears one's ears.
Sip after sip quenches your thirst. Enlivens a spirit. Refreshes a soul.
Run unabashedly naked with natural beauty through fields where tall
grasses grow. Become intoxicated by love itself. Let love enfold you.
Allow your sight to follow nature's trail from petal to stem, single
grass blade to root. Believe all to be your sisters and brothers.
Ponder and pine upon love's unending manifestations.
The things of life that really matter.
Acceptance and Forgiveness
Goodness and Compassion
Kindness and Courage
Purpose and Passion
Reason and Charity
Faith and Hope
Joy and Light
Peace and Wisdom
Happiness and Abundance
and you will discover Me.

TAKE TIME, DEAR ONE

Take time to hug a child, soften your scorn, see them smile and be reborn.

Take time to gaze above and see the sky and release your need to understand why.

Take time to climb a mountain, cross a sea and truly be all you can be.

Take time to greet someone you may not know for it is joy and love that you will sow.

Take time to help a friend with efforts to mend measures of strife that cut like a knife.

Take time to run and jump and dance and sing, each of these is a special thing.

Take time to cry and mourn, let go of pain, it is only then that we live again.

Take time to discern things to sincerely do for only then do dreams come true.

Take time to rest, relax and renew yourself or caring will cease for anyone else.

Take time to abandon what others have called a sin and discover instead the power within.

Take time in stillness for peace in mind, a gift of love to yourself, so kind.

MY JOURNEY

Am I on a journey to find Thee, oh God?
Nay, I have found Thee hidden, in the sanctuary of my soul,
beckoning me onward, pushing me forward
toward an eternal destiny.

What then is this road?
Where does it lead my wandering soul?
Could it be a journey of outer discovery?
Nay, for I see what lies in front of me.

It must be a road toward discovery of me.
So, that I may see behind these eyes,
the man I know,
my heart to be.

It must be a journey inward to the labyrinth of truth;
this path that I am on, this path of love,
to explore the farthest corners of my mind,
discovering the deepest desires of my dreams.

Searching across the hills and valleys of a lifetime,
peering through windows of my past, ever more deeply into myself.
Seeking the dark corners of my mind. Never fearing what I may find.

I am hoping to see for the first time, all of me;
the darkness and the light, the past and the potential,
the degradation and the perfection,
it is all a part of me, and I am proud.

Would I dare to reverse if I could, an error from my past?
No, neither time, nor my spirit, will allow.
Wisdom, accumulated through the years, lays in residual fears,
allowing me to see the man made from my past, inspired to be.

Each pitfall and provocation, challenge and scar, a badge of honor,
proclaiming to the world that I am human and Divine,
unfolding, seeking, opportunities to test my body,
my courage, my character, my faith, my mind.

Each apparent misstep, mistake, lapse in judgment and character,
all unconsciously, useful, providing for me the opportunity to grow.
What is this journey, if not a journey of discovery,
where my past greets my present and my future unfolds.

This journey that I take, this path that I am on,
contains excitement and thrills, disappointments, horrors and chills.
It is not for the faint of heart, nor weakness of will.
This journey, I must take alone, is one of discovery and uncovery.

Discovery of God, uncovery of me,
discovery of man all lie within, and ahead.
And so, I go.
My journey continues.

LISTEN TO ME

Listen to my voice. I give the guidance you need,

Don't fret upon the message. Success is guaranteed.

Follow each direction that comes into your mind,

but discern with good intentions, only those that are so kind.

You are meant to give of love, in harmony and joy,

free from all the pain, your prejudices may employ.

Listen to me always. I will always guide your ways,

For my love lasts forever, till the ending of your days.

IT TAKES FAITH

It is in the moments between breaths that I notice you
When my body must rely on faith
As I let loose of my life-saving air
And trust that you will be there

It is in between my foot falls that I have come to know
The assurance of your presence
As I let go of the ground beneath my feet
And step with faith refusing to retreat

In those times each day when I close my eyes
To blink or sleep for but a moment's time
As my shutters close, my sight concealed
It is with faith that I wait for the world revealed

And when my palm reaches out to another
For help, to appease or to be so kind
In those infinite moments when I wait for a hand to hold
It takes faith in love, your promise foretold

WHAT WOULD YOU DO?

If you saw me, would you love me,
      or beat me, bruise me, boundary me, or border me?

If you saw me, would you recognize me,
      or see me strange, call me names, denigrate or demonize me?

If you listened to me, would you hear me,
      or belittle and berate me, denounce and deny me?

You claim to want me and to follow me,
      but when I appear in your midst, do you see me at all?

BREATHE

Breathe.
The long day's journey into night is about to begin.
Delayed by relentless conversations and questions with one's mind.
Stop. Stop your chores. Stop your work. Stop your movement. Stop.

Night's whispers are calling you to slow and simply breathe.
Let the world spin of its own accord, out of control if it wishes.
It continues with or without you but will always call for your company.

Say *No*.
Lovingly, respectfully, retreat into a land of shadows and dreams.
Let the comfort of night warm and caress you with its velveteen cloak
of darkness, lulling you into a deep relaxing slumber with its sweet
melody of silence. Breathe.

Another world awaits your immanent arrival and immortal soul.
As night falls, dreams of a weary, restless mind call, beckoning you to
be its companion. The world of waking will get along without you,
though miss you dearly.

Journey now into a world of illusion, fantasy and dreams, the truest of
realities, where desires are fulfilled, demons are faced, fears conquered,
and the body rests, rejuvenated, reborn. Breathe.

Your passport to this new world? A simple breath.
So, breathe, into a body relaxing and a mind dissolvent of worrisome
thoughts. For the long day's journey into night has already begun.

EXPLORATION

Sparks flash, light streams, thrust into new, known, world.
Demons and dragons lie in wait, waiting patiently to be conquered.

Caverns and passages shrouded in the darkness of fear.
Paths to places yet unknown begging to be discovered and uncovered.

Emerging fertile fields budding, abundant with life,
as seedlings stretch, reaching with tender strength, for the light.

Fields covered and cultivated with manure,
deposited then discarded, yet necessary for the harvest.

Tears rain down within, washing away a thin layer of sadness, cradling
hope in a stream of comfort, creating pools that glisten with gratitude.

Man, earth, beast, light; all one. Down these brightly blackened
paths, across these barren, abundant fields, I discover me.

Nothing to fear, while terror reigns from time to time.
This inner terrain, familiar and foreign, waiting to be explored, is mine.

PRESSING ON

Down a dark, murky highway I travel.
Pushed, forced, called – it doesn't matter.
All that matters is movement.
I see little. My sight barely piercing the darkness.

Here and there along the way, I see light.
Insight guides my way.
I know not where I am going,
only that I can't go back.

Where am I going? Where are you leading?
The roadmap scribbled with lines in all directions
each offering a new adventure,
fading, yet converging, leading me in one direction, inward.

You say, *follow your compass*,
A tool that until recently I didn't know I had.
Its steadiness scares yet ensnares me.
I must follow and stay the course.

Dawn breaks on the horizon.
Landscapes of worldviews outstretch and beckon me.
I see other travelers on distant roads, all moving toward a
common destination and dream.

Each exchanging a knowing smile, a gift of assurance.
The road continues to rise up.
I press on.
The journey continues.

THE ARTISAN

Thoughts expressing, feelings evoked, patterns changing, the canvas of life awash with color, images emerge, creating a dazzling display and a story to tell, with each stroke depth is uncovered and discovered.

Care is given to carve the lines gently yet boldly across the cloth of my being, curving, creating shadows and contours of thought and behavior blending with a complexity of complimentary colors that reach out and in, to bring to life that which laid flat and lifeless until now.

Each concoction thoughtfully, intuitively mixed together to create a color combination unseen until now by this world, yet uniquely expressed in form. But continue it must, for the Master is precise and his vision is expansive and intricate. Each form has a story to tell. Each image evokes a thought and reaction from those near, and those who give their eyes time to rest upon and ponder the message.

Every image, a profound expression on this canvas of life. Constantly emerging in full color, continuously changing as other images are added to the painting and colors are mixed. The Artisan applies layer after layer taking time in detail, ensuring each has depth and meaning. A painting comes to life, striking a life-like pose engendered by spirit, capturing the attention of ages yet to come, transcending all boundaries, affirming the oneness of all mankind.

Each may look and all may see within themselves, that which is so skillfully sketched and created from the invisibility of the grand imagination, brought to life with fantastic flair, not meant to be hidden away or coveted by a few, but viewed and touched by many; shared with all, for all time.

The Master has formed a thought, transformed by imagination, colored by joy, placed expressively, skillfully, passionately upon the canvas. Each color and form, brushed with infinite love; created to tell a tale, ignite passion, enrapture a heart, and entice new thought. Each a masterpiece in and of itself. Everyone an original; a new creation of infinite beauty in the Artisan's mind.

I Am Here in the Midst of Fear

I thought that I had dealt with fears to date.
A friend spoke honestly and found me irate.

He did not speak to judge or offend,
but I, in turn, sought to defend

my actions, my thoughts, my ideas, my truth.
Each uncovering fears from my youth.

His words were just, and he spoke his heart.
In fear I responded, to separate, to part

from the conversation, the talk, the situation, the car,
believing perspectives were too distant, too far.

This is my response, to retreat, to end
conversations and interactions, instead of to mend.

The wisdom of spirit, its voice so near
ringing softly and gently, in my ear.

*"This is a fear you have, so be attuned
catch yourself, lest a friendship be ruined.*

*The arrogance you express, and stress inside
mask some fears that cannot be disguised.*

*Is it fear of wrong, not being good, or smart.
This fear you have hardens your heart.*

It closes your ears, eyes, and mind,
to the lessons of wisdom from friends you may find.

Each is a messenger with words so true,
offering opportunities, to step into you.

Be at peace, I am here, through friends so dear,
giving you grace and space free and clear,

of judgment, of error, of shadow and harm,
there is no reason for fear, angst, and alarm.

Chances will rise to face your fears,
Moment by moment through the years."

STRENGTH OF THE HEART

a shadow of darkness and despair shrouds my heart
clouding my mind fear rises within
strengthened and spurred on by short gasps for air
constricted by a heavy hand which will not hold
but presses, compresses,
trying to suppress   my Spirit

what does one, can one do but succumb to
this devil's hand allowing his attack to continue
stabbing and tearing at the lining of my heart
his minions erecting temporary walls
embankments which halt the reinforcements
of life from reaching   my Mind

let the battle rage for only awhile longer the
light at the end has already appeared
the war had been won before beginning
peace promised and prosperity foretold
the battle is over, pressure released,
power is mine, strength found within   my Heart

STRETCH ME

Stretch me
Make me twist and turn
Bend but never break me

For my mind can only see over the next hill
I need my brothers and sisters
To test me with their traits and troubles
So that I see what I am made of

Pull at my heart
It is malleable enough and enlarged enough
To enfold even my harshest of critics and
Those who are blinded by anger
Who only hear what will serve their fear

See, as I am stretched,
The bands of forgiveness and appreciation
That are contained within,
Bands of loving understanding
Held together by a centering faith that cannot be broken

Commit me to loving and serving others
To being a guide in troubled times
So that I may expand my consciousness
And open to new worlds of wonder within and without

RESIST NOT – A CONVERSATION WITH LIGHT

Resist not the pressures of life and pine not over the futile calls of an earthly mind. Habits and compulsions beckon you to come and settle for the self of old. Resist not the truth of your existence, the call of your heart, the answers in thought, the wisdom of mind, the flow of all that is, into your life.

Days and nights, like the fog roll in, blurring your hope, muddling your mind. You continue to step into the mist of have-to's, should-be's, I can'ts, and why me's, then wonder why and where you have lost yourself along the way.

Why will my mind not stop spinning like a disk stuck on perpetual play mode, shifting from track to track playing old tunes that I have now outgrown?

Why do the enemies of fortune continue to storm the gates of my mind, assaulting my will in their relentless attack?

Why do I give in, give up, move forward in life like an automaton, programmed to be grateful to just get by?

Why do I resist the flow, openness, opportunities, willingness to accept and receive new ideas, new gifts, new life?

Why do I resist the call to let go, clean the house of the self, move on, receive love, give love, accept my inheritance now, and welcome my just desserts at the table of life?

I tell myself that I am worthy yet.
I resist and worries persist.
I resist and my lack of self-worth exists.
I resist and tell the universe, it's okay to treat me as an afterthought.
I resist, finding myself groveling at the feet of humanity,
taking whatever scraps fall from the table of others.
Am I wrong?

This is wrong. It can't be right.

I hear a voice.
Resist not the peace that lies within.
Resist not the answers to all ponderances in life.
Resist not the call to stop and breathe.
Silence the madness in your mind and open the floodgates to
your heart and your hands and receive.
I cannot give to you what you will not receive,
that which you don't believe.
All that you should, can and ought to receive.
Just believe.

My mind is conditioned to continue to resist.
I don't want to hear, for I have grown comfortable with my mania.
Don't you understand? It is all I know.

You are wrong, dear one.
There within you, lay the answers. More peace, harmony, happiness,
more avenues of abundance and prosperity than you have allowed
yourself to believe and receive. You bask in the limited habits of your
hands and thoughts and resist the Truth. Abandon them, not I.

Resist not I, nor what is rightfully yours, nor all that is stored up in
and for you, in heaven and on earth. There are no contracts or
conditions that must be signed or fulfilled.

No challenges that cannot be overcome as you welcome with open
arms your inheritance right here, right now.
Simply open to the flow of life, of the universe, of Me.

Allow it to overflow in you and spill into your life,
filling it with achieved dreams, and effortless abundance.

Choose now to receive.
Lay down your man-made defenses and resist not.

I Am Your Screams

I bellow…*HELP ME. I Am in PAIN. Hear My SCREAMS.*

Among the deafening din of wails within, I hear…
I Am your screams
I scream for love
I scream for justice
I scream for longing
I scream for health
I scream for touch
I scream for assurance
I scream for safety
I scream that I may be seen
I scream so the entire world will hear

I scream about poverty
I scream about disparity
I scream about inequity
I scream about injustice
I scream about unfairness
I scream against false prophets
I scream against the self-righteous
They give nothing to those unlike them
Let me scream through you so all will see and hear Me.

Make them give love
Make them be just
Make them quench thirst
Make them be well
Make them embrace
Make them respond
Make them protect all
Make them see Me in others
Make them hear Me in you

I Am you.
I speak to you and through you, in all, all ways.
The question is will you scream?
Will you scream loud enough so they will hear Me in your screams?

My pain subsides. I have been heard.
I gather my breath and get ready to scream!

TRAPPED WITHIN

Spirit, a waxened, reflective face
shifts within my soul,
positioning itself for maximum advantage,
ever-present at every turn.

No running.
No escape.
In this labyrinth
At every turn I see you.

Trapped in love, wisdom,
insight, and courage,
all things foreign yet familiar,
thrust upon me at every turn.

You trap me.
Forcing me to
be, at depth,
who I already am.

STRETCH

I will stretch

I will stretch to see you in light
with my mind guided right
when perception and illusion distort my sight

I will stretch to look past
the shadow that fears shall cast
enfolding you in love and forgiveness that lasts

I will stretch with impatience
when my minds settles into complacence
and my will defaults to complaisance

I will stretch with faith when on this soul's journey hides
the answers to loss that will ease each of my strides
knowing in love's presence peace resides

I will stretch

Q&A

I walk alone and ask,
Won't you give me a little something, God,
so I can continue along my journey?

I hear thoughts in my mind, audible in kind,
You may have all that is mine;
All there is.

I stop.
A thoughtless *thank you* is offered within my mind.
I begin to walk on.

Wait, you have not answered, a voice calls out.
Will you take what I have to offer?
Will you take all there is?

I stop for a moment, paralyzed by fear, not by the voice of
God, but by the answer that I must rear. I pause, allowing the truth of
God to rise in me, pressing me to stake my claim right here, right now.

YES! I will take all that I need.
Should I hoard it, grab it, steal it away? I wonder.
No, I will accept all, in all forms.
I used to think myself unworthy, think thoughts
sparingly and poor, use only that which I
desperately needed, now I am offered what
I truly desire and I say, YES!

Can I reach out with open hands that would mirror my
open mind and grateful heart?
Will I take and receive all of the somethings that God is willing to give?
My mind says, *YES!*
Will my hands follow suit?
Wait and see.

PART III

GIFTS FROM STANDING IN THE LIGHT

LOVE AND PRESENCE

Love is present and presence is love.
Intertwined in purpose and meaning.
Inseparable, one from the other.
Each is one and the same.

You cannot yearn for one and neglect the other.
For you will be lost in a world
of missed-giving and misunderstanding.
You cannot find one without being the other.

IN THE VACUITY OF GOD

There is a vacuity within me
Where God is born anew and renewed
From time to time

When I take time to cease
The frantic fight and rapid speed
To force the world upon myself

Gulfs open wide within
Water rises to open skies
And God appears in me

From the voluminous silence
Presence echoes everywhere
And I hear the call of Spirit near

Through the canyons of my soul
I am called forth
To mingle, co-mingle, with God-Myself once more

ASK FOR NOTHING

I asked for fewer and fewer things.

Then a voice was heard within,

> *Ask for nothing and you*
> *will see, I have given you*
> *everything.*

Now I calmly, patiently,
sit in silence, and alas

I see All.

LOVE IS

Love is ever present, ever flowing.
Love is power, passion and purpose within each person.
Love is the mind transcending ignorance, apathy and anger.
Love is Spirit's spark that sets hearts afire.
Love is all there is.

For what else is there but love?
No power is greater, no force stronger.
No material more valuable or plentiful.
It alone lifts you to insurmountable heights,
From its roots born and buried in the deepest recesses of your soul.

For love is all things. It is the beauty that rises in sight.
It is the peace that calms restless souls.
It is the sound of laughter that brings joy to life.
It is the hope that reigns eternal in human hearts.
It is I in the fullness of who I am, and the allness of you.

Love is the very breath of life.
In sum, love, simply, is.

WHISPER ON THE WIND

I see the branches in the trees move and the leaves shimmer as an unseen force presses between each stem and against the sturdiness of the trunk. I see nothing with my eyes, yet I hear,

> *"It is I"* whispered on the wind.

I see waves of grass in fields of gold bend and sway as a steady breath blows across the tips of hair tussled atop each blade. Petals on wildflowers in the meadow become buoyant in the breeze. I see nothing that demonstrates such gentle power, yet I sense presence itself, and hear,

> *"It is I"* whispered on the wind.

I watch birds and butterflies rise high in the sky. Their wings outstretched, uplifted by an invisible force. They fly, glide and float held aloft by an invisible hand. I see no hand nor understand the nature of flight, yet I believe that all is possible, for I hear,

> *"It is I"* whispered on the wind.
> *I am the spirit that lifts.*
> *I am the force bending and bowing to design.*
> *I am the stream that sways.*
> *I am the visible and unseen for which only trust is required.*

I turn within and suddenly hear, *"It is I"*, whispered on the wind.

KNOW LOVE

Love, so clear,
seems far but yet so near.
Reaching out to receive its embrace,
and catch the glimmer of its face.

Waiting for you to return its glance.
Hoping that it has the slightest chance,
for a moment, season or lifetime romance.
Love invites you to join its dance.

Silent, hopeful, beating strong.
Love lasting, lifetimes long.
Taste it, feel it, smell its scent.
Love's aroma, heaven sent.

Do not tarry in this hour.
Do not wait to feel love's power.
Immerse yourself and hear love's thunder.
Transfix your heart and know love's wonder.

HEALTHY AND WHOLE

I am healthy and whole.

No person, disease or thought can convince me otherwise. My body, in its vain attempt, uses clever ploys to infect me with its feelings and sensations of fatigue, trying to trick me into settling, with age, for something less than perfection. A master trickster it is.

My mind, an illusionist unto its own, both feeds and foils my body's plans for domination. Together they cavort and secretly collaborate, but their collusion is uncovered, exposed, by Spirit.

So powerfully does it move in and through me, expanding the truth of my wholeness, revealing the secrets to my body's strengths and my mind's power, breaking down the walls of doubt that I am, or could ever be, anything less than whole

This, my birthright my ace in the hole, the knowledge that I am healthy and whole.

TRUTH TOLD

Life, abundant, flowing, loving,

Love witnessing, accepting, expressing,

Wisdom teaching, listening, knowing,

Mind seeing, sensing, glowing,

Heart feeling, hoping, assuring,

Body healing, outstretching, enshrining,

World entwining,

Spirit shining

Human kindness realigning,

All Divine.

Avatar – Your True Self

A being not of this world, ability beyond comprehension,
power beyond measure, you are an Avatar,
an incarnate creature and teacher of the Divine.

Beauty beyond compare, a fire burns in your heart.
The fire of Spirit, of passionate love.
For all that is and can possibly be, is in you.

Let the fire scorch you, burning away the
falseness of limitation, and the façade of
this temporary reality, in which humanity dwells.

Let the fire seer the skin of your ego,
exposing the soft, tenderness of your Spirit.
Let it warm your heart and enlighten your mind,
as you take the embers, using them to ignite the fire in your soul.

Blow it, stoke it, set it ablaze.
All who are allowed to touch you, hear you, be near to you,
can touch the fire within.
Let them be feel its warmth or be burnt by your truth.

Let them touch the essence of your being and find themselves.
Kindred spirits, the timbers have been felled. The coals await.
The heavenly hearth ready, waiting to ignite the fire within,
so, you may finally be your true self in this new world.

REALITY

The long night of slumber comes to an end.
I awake to a world unknown, undiscovered,
infinitely real to the mind, to the touch.
A world that has always been, yet unseen by
me, in me. Changed by thought, not of what
is but what I will it to be. What I hold, in
mind, produces after its kind. What I believe
to be, manifests and I see, all of the fears I
have created, all of my wants kept at a
distance. Unable until now to wrap my mind
around the reality within. Unaware of the
power I wield.

The call goes out and echoes within
       Think it
       Speak it
       See it
       Feel it
       Taste it
       Act it
       Live it
       Be it

And so it is, and so it shall be.
For I already Am, in reality.

A Seed is Planted

In every moment a seed of understanding opens and life bursts forth,
    That seed is life, and that life is good.

From this tiny seed a great vine will grow and from its branches
    buds and blossoms of love, wisdom, faith and hope will bloom.

Each will grow prolifically, sinking its roots into heart and mind,
    spreading across the consciousness of humans and all-kind.

Let it grow watering it with the oxygen of wisdom so all shall taste its
    fruit, tethered by its roots, and strengthened by its vine.

See, the seed lies within the rich hubris of life. Till the soil each morn.
    Nurture its growth with works of hands and heart in equal fashion.

THIS IS PRAYER

To touch the face of God
with a single thought
and hear the Word in mind.

To silence my mind
and hold my tongue
so that I may hear wisdom's voice.

To feel eternal bliss this day,
enraptured by love
streaming into my heart.

To dwell in heavenly thoughts
immersed in truth, allowing life itself
to be me and flow through me.

To live a life so human
guided by the grace of the Divine
touching others with endless compassion.

To forget myself
and bend to the will of goodness
and be molded by its hands.

This is prayer.

THE TRUTH – A CONVERSATION WITH SELF

I say to you, this is the Truth:

I am cosmic in consciousness and Christ-like in power
I am infinite in being, expanding beyond the moons of Pluto and farther
      than the distant stars
I am timeless, birthed before the heavens and ageless beyond eternity
I am the creation of the Creator. By my hand creation continues or
      chaos reigns
I am the essence of all life, and all life dwells within me
I am man, woman, soil, earth, water, sky, creature of every kind seen
      and unseen, known and unknown by my race
I am love's eternal embrace and compassionate kiss on bended knee for
      all humanity
I am God incarnate, a deliverer of souls, a spirit of light
I am everywhere present at once for all,
I am one in God, and God is one, as me.

This is the Truth. As me, I Am.

THE IMMANENCE OF ME

Impending light,
blinding bursting in sight.
Immeasurable power in my soul
to wield and sling and take control
of wayward thoughts of man so small,
transfiguring each with the All.
No more am I able to hide
from infinite love that dwells inside.
Wisdom, fortune in universal proportion,
abide within from a cosmic consortium.
No excuse nor doubt is left to be.
Now that I have discovered the immanence of me.

THE PAINTER'S PALETTE

Be what you see. The painter's palette lies within you.
Life is your canvas.
See the colors of your dreams laid out before you.

Yours to use, touch, mix and spread across the canvas of life.
Allow them to color your emotions, your thoughts, your words.
Feel the power in each color of the painter's palette.
> The passion of one
> The energy of another
> The potency of all within, to be spread throughout.

You are the creator
The painter of the portrait that the world will see.
> What is it you see?
> What do you wish to be?

The brush is ready, your canvas awaits.

LOVE LIKE THE SUN

Love – like the rising of the sun.

Allow it to burst forth in your heart and blaze in your mind,
   Shining through your eyes
   Settling on your tongue
   Radiating from your touch

Streaming outward
   Warming a heart
   Helping a friend
   Healing a soul.

SHINE

Dazzling
Sunlight
Blinding
Beautiful
Starburst
Glistening
Exploding
Radiant

Streaming into Consciousness

Words cannot capture nor a heart express
that which a mind barely comprehends
All that you are.

Simply, remember and continue to shine!

That Which I Am

I am Good.

Goodness itself is the essence of my being.
No evil lurks within, no darkness shadows the brilliance of my being.
No dragons fly from my mind to scare
nor scorch the earth or its peoples.

I am goodness and light.

My dazzling display of energy and unbridled display of passion for
men, women, all people blinds most folk who are used to shielding
their eyes from their own brilliance. My light is unbounded, radiating
from my touch, my smile, my heart, and my personhood.
Unseen by the naked eye, it streams into consciousness. Too bright for
some, its illumination and warmth welcomed by others.
It cannot be controlled or toned down, for it is outside of my control.
The power streams from that which is within and beyond.
It is my job to simply shine.

I am goodness, light and love.

My love is sacred and universally shared. Though directed man to man through the sensuality of my intimate connections, and spread to all in word and deed, fulfilling my personal mission and public role, it is all one and the same. Love cannot be changed or differentiated, diminished by who it is directed at nor by its intended purpose. Love is the bailiwick of no person or place or plan. It is original in nature, universal in purpose, unable to be restricted to a few, refined by some, or withdrawn from others. Love simply is – present in all, the essence of all – in me.

I am goodness, light, love and all that is.

In me, God is goodness and all that is; all that ever has been – the genes of Spirit, the potential of humanity at its best. Inheriting the hopes of creation, driven by the mind of the One, buoyed by the assurance of life in all its forms – the energy that underlies all – I am that which some fear, that which others misunderstand, that which some hold at arm's length, but that which all desire. Come, touch me. Touch my consciousness, be healed by my words, find comfort in the humble power of my presence. Have no fear of me. All that is, is in me – and in you.

AFTER THOUGHTS

Never, in my early life, did I entertain the thought that I would write anything, let alone poetry. But I fell in love with poetry decades ago while in high school.

The joy, goal, and now need to write came from always sensing a call to express messages that *came to me* inside. Throughout my life, entire discourses on subjects, rebuttals to articles I've read, poems in their entirety, or entire curriculums for teaching would unfold in my mind. If I quieted my mind, more would unfold.

I would read the works of others – articles, books, poetry, periodicals – and challenge myself to do whatever someone else did, with that which I felt was mine to express. If someone else wrote a poem, I would humbly but confidently believe, "I think I can do that too." If someone wrote an intriguing or provocative article, I would think, "I'm going to try that too because I think this or that should be said too." I remember reading some articles in newspapers offering daily spiritual guidance. I thought, "I think I should do that. There are perspectives that are not being offered. Maybe it's supposed to be me who is to offer daily spiritual guidance. I don't know how to do it, but I'll try the best I can, to help whoever I can." So, I studied the form and format of writing news articles, condensing large lessons into 100-500 words. I selected a few topics that I thought would be relevant and which I could speak to. I turned within, to contemplation and meditation, to listen and find my voice. The voice with which readers may resonate. I submitted my articles to various newspapers and magazines. Lo and behold, they were picked up by four newspapers.

I would read poetry in books and magazines, journals and placards on buses and trains. At one point I thought, "I can see everything that these poets see – every moment and nuance of life and emotion – an expanse of time caught in a single stanza. I think I can do that too." So, I studied various forms of poetry. Then, took refuge in quiet spaces and within nature whenever I could. I let light stream into me, and I began composing. I submitted poems to a few journals and to various collections. Three were accepted in the first two years.

In the following years, I found myself composing rhymes for children's books, meditations for audios, and business book manuscripts. I couldn't stop writing. The light of inspiration, motivation, imagination, and service had been turned on in me. The stream was continuous as I opened myself to it. I share all this with you, my friends, because the stream is not meant for only a few of us. The stream engulfs all of us. We must merely be open to it.

It does not matter what you call your light source: God/god, Buddha, Mother, Gaia, Spirit, etc. The list of names and rules of religions from countless cultures, traditions, and paths matter not. Write each day. Express in your own way to people who will resonate with your version of a word. Seek not to proselytize or proclaim in attempts to convert or convince others. Use words that bring comfort to yourself and to others. Your awareness, your ecstasy of experience, your journey to enlightenment, your revelations are yours alone. Make your path personal, for the prism of people's eyes and minds splits light, and no one sees light in the same way. Each of us must be a stream of light unto others.

When you turn within or without, seeing only through the lens of love, understanding, beauty, and compassion, then light will stream into you and move through you. You, too, will become a stream of light for this world.

So, my friends, I invite you to read or listen to *Light Stream*. Let each poem or piece of prose speak to you long after your eyes have wandered from the page. May you be a light stream for others in your midst.

-   Rob Schout

ABOUT THE AUTHOR

Robert Schout – poet, author, column contributor to newspapers and journals, business consultant, personal/professional life coach, leadership and management skills expert, and organization effectiveness specialist – believer in dreams. Robert Schout has dedicated his life to service, first as a social worker, then visiting professor, spiritual teacher, organization consultant and executive coach, and now as an author and poet. He has heard the voice and words streaming into consciousness of dozens of books and hundreds of poems over the years, always taking notes, scribbling words and phrases to remember, on thousands of pieces of paper. Finally completing collections of nature poems, spirit-inspired poetry, and LGBTQ poetry, and offering them, as he has his service, to the world.

Published poems by Robert James Schout

Timeless Voices, 2005
-   "Let Me Hide"

Sacred Journeys, 2007
-    "Amongst the Junipers and Pines"

Scenes from the Live Poet's Society, 20th Anniversary, Vol. IV, 2011
-    "The Breath of Dawn"
-    "Restless Gaze"
-    "Rain"
-    "God's Answer"
-    "Droplets of Water"

2017 Winner: Ross Andrews Nature Poem Contest – "In the Shadows of a Morn"

Schout It Out LLC Publications and Products

I Can Illustrated Children's Books

- *What Can I See Today*
- *What Can I Do Today*
- *What Can I Say Today*
- *What Can I Give Today*

Listen: Nature's Wisdom in Poetic Form

Shout Outs@Work™: Employee Appreciation Note Cards

Turning and Returning: Guided Meditations for Gaining Insight. (Audio Book)

Schout It Out Greeting Card Collections
- Winter Scenes Collection
- Piece of Heaven Collection
- Street Art Collection
- Sea Life Collection
- Coloring Card Collection for Kids

Visit *Schout It Out LLC* for more information
www.schoutitout.com
schoutitout@gmail.com

PowerSkills Training & Development Inc Seminars and Services

Rob Schout is President of PowerSkills Training & Development, Inc.

PowerSkills Everywhere Seminars

PowerSkills offers more than 50 online and onsite courses and seminars focused on a wide range of professional, organization, and management development skills.

PowerSkills Micro-Training Classes

PowerSkills offers more than 30 micro-training classes on a variety of professional development, leadership development, life skills, and life-enrichment lessons and strategies.

PowerSkills Coaching and Advising

PowerSkills offers personal growth, professional goal achievement, management insight-orientation, and executive advisory coaching services by its team of certified coaching professionals.

Visit *PowerSkills Inc.* to request copies of catalogs
www.powerskillsinternational.com
info@powerskillsinternational.com

www.ingramcontent.com/pod-product-compliance
Lightning Source LLC
Chambersburg PA
CBHW071020120626
46546CB00003B/1174